This (Boi)yant Body

Narratives of a queer Black boi & the
waters that carry them.

Autobiographical recounts of

Bobbi Kindred

Conviction 2 Change LLC
www.conviction2change.com

This (Boi)yant Body

Edition 2018

Published by Conviction 2 Change LLC
www.conviction2change.com

Library Congress Control Number: 2018948113
ISBN: 0692140123
ISBN-13: 978-0692140123

Cover Design: Chris "L7" Cuadrado
IG: @Lsiete7
forthepueblo@gmail.com

Editor: Taylor D. Duckett
IG: @C2Cpublishing
Conviction2change@outlook.com

for my inner child I mother,

the parts of myself deserving our forgiveness

& the wounds within us all that still gape

Foreword

These unpublished words were eating at my spirit. It was as though I was trying to actively burry parts of myself I considered to be too shameful to share. There is no hiding from the truth once it has escaped my thoughts and bled itself on paper; not only must I face it, but the world gets to hold me accountable for those truths.

This (Boi)yant Body is an ode to my Black boihood, my inner child, and the water that has returned us to ourselves countless times. This work, born in the spirit of needing an out from the depths of learned self-hatred, is a detailed account of my transition from being raised and displaced in the suburbs of San Ramon, CA., to the utter tiredness over living out the patterns of addiction that lead me into drug and alcohol recovery. It is only a surface scratch, and I am grateful for the opportunity to give you all insight on my internal process through sharing work that stems from 2013 onward.

With God's Consent,

Cierra Green, Bobbi Kindred, Jolinda's Baby

I took a life to give a life
That is what's nice
January 13th was the day she was born
It was rainy
Stormy
Yet a little warm
When I looked at her she had a charm
She looked me in the eye and said
"Momma a star is born"
So I welcome you into this world
Say hello to my star, Cierra,
My baby girl

Jolinda Givens, Mama

What the Water Gave Me

all i've ever known was feet staying miles a w a y
from ocean's homicidal mouth
swallowing-whole Black bodies who dared to dip their —

"nigger, don't go tryna escape in the water or you'll be corpse dusted!"

"baby, don't swim in the water or you will
***become** the water!"*

so my calloused ankles stay shackled on ~~shore~~ sureness
sand particles clutching the cracks my toes,
gripping at my ankles:

> they
> know
> i'm
> never
> leaving.

have you ever tried running through sand?
ankles gripped like an abusive lover who can't stand to see you
leave?
but if you don't break

towards

freedom

you'll forever be stuck in a body
that will never really belong to you
so long as you stay stagnant in their grip.

all i've known is standing stuck; stagnant
reflective gazes in oceans not recognizing myself.
these legs — all battered, beaten, sand flea bitten.

this body – all dressed in sundress cut knee high.
me – all disguising myself in an identity
i hardly identified with.

        i look like woman would some days
      but i know i am no woman most days.

all i've known is bones shaking at the sight of the fluid.
fear incited on the thought of becoming fluid.
of being an agentic ocean moving between all ~~shores~~ sureness.

all i've ever known was not knowing how to stay afloat
in a body that is flooding on the inside.
not knowing how to breathe when water starts leaking
uncontrollably out my eyelids,

           at the mere reflection of myself.
choking on what feels like the atlantic
      through my throat
    rising up,
i too am afraid of the fluid inside of me.

do you ever feel gender-

          less

           some days?

feel the woman-

     less-

        ness

         of your sway?

the man-

    less-

      ness

         of your soul?

like scattered

         misplaced

water

        droplets,

            wanting nothing more than

      to

        evaporate

              towards

        heaven

so when a god and all his aryan angels look at you with disgust
and closes the gates on *your kind*,
at least you will be spat

      back

        down as rain

        and be embraced by all the other bodies

        who corrected god's mis-gendering mouth.

"nigger don't dare get in water you'll get bodied!"

        "no baby!" Mama's scared-self screamed*;*
          "my baby girl,
          they hunt for bodies like you!
          don't leap in that water,
          the fish hooks are **nooses!***"*

i took a leap in the water and cried,
    "massa', you can't hold me with your shackles!"

cried,
    "Mama, let me show you this buoyant body!"

Mama, you birthed a baby of all-water,

              all-fluid,
            all-malleability,

watch me change shapes

like water, Mama,
watch my hormones
shapeshift
watch my body embrace this fluidity
watch my ankles bust through and break

free

from being shackled in woman's body.

watch my fleshy fluid self claim the identity
you warned me to be afraid of!

i's can swim Mama.
i's can swim Mama,
i's can swim Mama
at least in this body,

i's can now swim.

I used to sit alone in my room
Listening to snails glide across the pavement
Leaving behind slimy residue
I've known the muffled cries of hummingbirds,
& toe tips of arachnids lurking on the rooftop corners
And when no one else was home,
I'd scream out my own name as loud as I could
And pretend the echoes were you
Calling out for me.

2:37 A.M.

my restless eyes burn
adjusting to the oppressive blackness
of this sleepless monday mourning
2:37 a.m.

      i am alone
      i am lonely.

desperately seeking comfort
i text you –
privileged enough to attain sleep.

two minutes later,
a follow up text

      i love you
        sleep well.

i won't tell you i'm lonely and alone.

you don't belong to me.
i share you with what feels like a million men,
and all your love and attention i receive

                part time

is *usually* enough for me.

i scroll through instagram,
the same feed keeps appearing
i stare blankly at the screen
like an entity stripped of its five senses,
if emptiness was one of them,
then that would fully encompass me.

i actively search for love through cyberspace;
it's nearly impossible to believe
that i can actually be loved
     by a real human being.
i spend my time messaging any remotely potential
                                      on okcupid,
it's the only thing that keeps me believing.
when I come across a match with over fifty-percent matching,
                  that's enough for me.

my eyes don't see good women
because good women are not good enough.
to them,
i am jeffrey dahmer,
devouring their savory souls like the last supper.

i'd much rather have my body
be labeled "fragile, handle with care",
                  then bombarded by bulls,
bomb my nagasaki,
                      sock me where it hurts
fuck me
                      and fuck me over
slit my body into uneven halves
          done by half-assed measurements of affection
screw drive through my body
            and steal the light shining through me

i'm okay with that,
because i am lonely
     and undeserving.

am i deserving of the kind of love that never leaves?
or does my pickiness lead me to pick apart greatness,

though greatness i can't see in my own self.

i lie in my bed and marvel over my dream woman.
she'd be nature itself,
>   healing and beautiful,
>   strong and empathetic,
>   a feminist in fact,
she'd wear birkenstocks and backpack in the outback,
and her love for me would be evident.

she'd love me with words and actions.
she'd hate when i'm gone too long
so she'd send texts that read,
"where are you?
>   why are you not replying?
>   answer me! now!
>   i'll kill myself if you don't reply!"

and i'd reply.
and tell her she's fucking crazy.
i'd act like i hate how crazy she is.
but i'd love it secretly.

i'll know she loves me when she'll take her nails
and drag them across my face,
or smash my head against the wall,
verbally abuse my five foot five
so i'll stand two
>   inches
>   tall
and she'd kiss me after.

she'd be so good to be true,
that i'd provoke the violence

                    and broken   silence,
                        and mirrors,
        and windows,
                and hearts,
                        and souls.

when dawn comes creeping through the windows
and we are exposed by the eyes of the light,
we'd go on hikes,
and visit schools to teach young girls about self-respect
and shit like safe sex,
we'd spend our holidays with the poor,

                                who are richer than us,
handing them food as we do our great deeds –
not because of recognition
but because we'd genuinely be compassionate women
who'd love the world more than we could ever love ourselves.
like zoo animals we'll be prisoners,
enslaved to each other.
the obsessiveness will tell us
            we are not alone.

her arms will be tangled in my body
her grip will hug me tighter than unreceived hugs
and loves absence
than warmth that never made its way to me,
that reached them, *there*, and stayed.
never came my way.

I had to distill my wishes to its essence
The Universe, graciously,
Has always granted me my grief.

The 13-Year-Old Living In Us

she stands in the mirror
and it sounds too much like a dial tone,
like a you have reached the number of 5-1-0
the whole house ruptures in wail
and clash of furniture
flimsily glued together.
photos of store bought families in gold frames
quarrel with a f l u n g godey's lady's book.
a startled voice whispers
fool chil' you gon' wake massa' and miss's up
but she keeps collecting wallpaper in her fingernails.
and when all the fragments of glass shards scale the floor
she pounces on them
like puddles of mamas faintly remembered cry
& wonder if it still count as hurt if she is the only witness.
wonder if she still Black if there be no more mirrors.
and at 21,
this will be the best understanding of displacement
from our African diasporic roots
that we will know.

Midnight

twelve-year-old boy
rich ebony-skinned prince
which no one knew his name
but sneered calling out

"midnight"

when they saw him.
i refused to act as if he was kin
so i too asked him why his skin was purplish blue
and addressed him as midnight too.
each time he'd smile with our pain filled eyes.

the only thing that could assuage my rage
let alone pain
was laughter.

I held my fist up for Black Pride
Only to unfold my hands to the not-so- pigmented side
And I was more confused than ever.
Through my eardrum I caught the constant slick tongues
Of those who dare exchange racist insults
Which was not uncommon in my classes of twenty
With only two *lone* Black folks

                              Who dared not sit together.

White suburban america
Where you'd catch the colored kids hiding in the shadows
Where dark tint was acceptable
Refusing to expose their melanin where the light glows.

A Seat at the White Girls' Table/On Wednesdays We Lie

my daddy is italian,
i'd brag to my circle of cerulean eyed friends
with lazy blonde hair
that always seemed to effort-

              less-

                 ly fall

                     past their shoulders

he is half white,
which makes me part right.
pass the napkins, please.

On Wendy Brown's Wounded Attachments

To understand myself as Black, is to understand my Blackness to always be relational to whiteness/ is to understand my terms of freedom to be inextricably bound to a possibility that has been constructed for me to aspire to obtain/ is to have chains around my ankles that were never severed/ is to speak about myself and my abducted ancestors in a tongue forced into my mouth/ is to pass on generations of lashes and scars, embedded in skin that has never known any other name/ is to be captured and released and captured and released by the same set of hands.

They Called Us New

Baby,
Before there was *Black*
There was you.
After there is Black
There you will be, still.

Ain't that the greatest origin story never told.

MacArthur Station, 7 Years Old

what i learned from witnessing a Black woman get brutally
beaten by her spouse in public, with no bystander intervention:

the rule of *minding owns business* wasn't unique to our home.

this sort of tight-lip is hard forgotten.

dear body,
you are more than the black blue underneath fingertips
or the extension of arms lashing like whips
on the surface of your skin –
breaking like vocal chords screamed two seconds too long.

you never deserved to be enslaved to fear.

to have your hands and knees submerged in ground
treating her insecurities like gold in gravel
picking them up to show her her high value.
you crafted her statue to stand tall above the men that devalued
her.
and I know calloused hands had grown too tired.

body,
you are more than red indication of blood that signals stop.
or relentless hands never letting up
more than piercing screams in cars with steering wheels
trekking towards the sides of roads
 "i'll kill us both" she screamed
and i don't blame you for pleading for her to just do it.

but what has come of you,
you coy and cautious child
too cowardly to rise.
i dare you to rise.
i dare you to ascend yourself,
as you have ascended her.

No More Auction Block For Me

my mother would've been sick
if she'd seen how proud i was

                      to hold hands with a white girl.
how my backbone extended tall and erect
when we walked hands-clasped,
through "whites only" neighborhoods.
anglo pavements,
where fifteen-year-old me tucked kinky hair
underneath baseball caps & oversized black hoodies.

                    a place where i learned to negate my
                    blackness,
as if i could be read as anything other than
                Black

                                in their eyes.

since white-blonde girls were my unsung reflections in mirrors
i figured,
           being loved by one
                would *at least* get me closer to the whiteness
                    never written on my own skin.

on the first night she introduced me to her father,
           "daddy, this is my girlfriend"
his blue eyes bucked wide,
flashing words that read "whites only"
segregation split his mouth wide open
and i could hear the jump jim crow in his baritone.

his eyes held that same gawking,
same spit-to-face disgust of all generations
who too, would have disapproved of his

18

daughter's love for a negro girl.
would have wedged borders between our bodies,

                                        with *my* severed limbs,

as a reminder of the strange fruit
that comes of fancying america's emblem
                        of innocence and purity.

 i watched his daughter—my partner,
scurry to pick his disapproval off the ground
as she lists out reasons as to why *i*
wasn't like all the *other* Black kids they must have talked about
during family dinners:

   "daddy, she writes poetry, and she dances, she may even show you some of
                        her moves!"

this would be first time i recognized this body, to not be body at
all.
to be flesh,
object,

            a product,

              a package,

                    a marionette dangling upon her fingers

                            showing me off to her daddy

as if my blackness needed an explanation,
an asterisk that read "white-friendly

                        special,

                        talented,

                        not-a-thug,

                        trained,

acceptable to bring around during christmas time,
that non-threatening kind of blackness"

it was like nothing,
the rhetoric of 1865 insidiously familiar to her tongue –
                        sold!
her voice broke, suddenly,
from sound of suburban blonde
to auction block auctioneer,
*"y'all, this nigger writes poetry, and she dances, show them your moves,
nigger!"*
                        sold!

the ground shakes thunderously below me
the slate tiles on the kitchen floor beneath my feet turned
                  worn wooden plank—a platform—a block
and my limbs are moving – **sold!**
suddenly jigging –   **sold!**
jiving –   **sold!**
feet shuffling to an unsung gospel.

a whole audience now,
            of white relatives,
            of dublin,
            of livermore,
            of pleasanton,
            of san ramon,
            of santa cruz,
consumptive white bodies screaming
            *"dance nigger, dance, dance,
            haaaaa, dance, haaaaa, dance!"*

mid-dance, my shirt flies upward,
exposing the sort of ripe-ready breast
barring the sweetest milk her father ever longed for –
                        sold!
flesh bends over forward,

all black crescent moon ass out,
call it a cup holder –

sold!

i hear him ask,
"is it true black women have enlarged clitorises" –
"hell, there's only one way to find out" –

sold!

> *"daddy she writes poetry, and she dances,
> she may even show you some of her moves."*

her daddy's formerly gritted teeth turned pleased,
erecting the most carnivorous smile flesh had ever seen.

it would be years later til i ever stopped dancing
because to be a Black girl displaced in the suburbs
is to want nothing more than to disappear
and my god,
those white folks had such a way of making me feel
like the most exceptional,

> jigaboo dancing,
> special black girl

> they ever did see.

Afrika Dances On My Head

ashy-foot Black bitch
looking nothing like, and everything like me
Black.
insulting.
kicking, swaying
catching my fro between her toes –

    "stop dancing!
      your movement is not welcome,
      your jiving body is the reason my hair won't relax!"

inconsiderate of space
an untamed embarrassment –

    "i am not amused by this frequent movement,
      it's causing my hair to tangle and kink!
      you make me ugly with your dark melanin pigment
                    trailing on the tracks of your feet!
      you make my blonde hair dirty
      before the boys could even notice how pretty i can be!
          who would want a white woman
          with a slave dancing on her head anyway!?"

eyes stare at her in the mirror throwing salty glares
racist diction insulting her every being
so she would no longer find strength to dance her dance.
like the white masters beat her black skin
till her body lay flat on the thistle cotton fields
i plastered the Afrikan lands of my hair

                with chemical
                  remedy
          to hide all my black insecurities

                                        so i would appear to be
                                        more mixed-raced

no not as good as white

                                                    but hell,

                    even a mulatto was alright.

at least it looked like i bared the blood of beauty.

but after that six week chemical remedy faded,
Afrika again, rose from my scalp
as my roots grew in
fiercely she once again began to dance her dance.
the endless thuds booming
                from the bongos
                        caused her body to jive more quickly
                    rapidly,
                    entangling my hair with her clumsy ass feet!

 "if you must be up there can you at least sit quietly?
  because who would want a white women with a slave
  wreaking havoc on the top of her head?"

i was ashamed of her,
how dare she'd be deeply pigmented
                        and happy
                        all at once.

she then began to inspire me,
despite every effort to rape Afrika of her beauty
through trying to tame and restrain her with white chemical
cruelty

                    she had her own agenda.
there was no stopping her sways and kicking
                        and bold and beautiful

she set me free.
Afrika comforted me when i was given the rude awakening
that *i am Black*
and there was no purpose to conforming to a community
who oppressed my people in the first place.
she grew on me.

now her dance is the impetus behind my poetry
she is my contemplation
the rhythmic wonder bleeding out on my blank pages
her melanin is my muse
and her dance is an amalgamation of culture,

strength,
struggle,
and resilience.

i embrace this melanin laced ancestry
midnight essence,
dawn dew presence
washed over me
looking every day at my queen
jiving, moving, unstoppable.
i let my roots speak to me
and i will forever be
the woman who dances with Afrika,
on the top of her head.

A Solo Libation Ceremony

i swear they were coming,
perhaps they ran outta gas on the way to the scene.
i'm sure,
they were somewhere stranded on some side of some road
angered that they, yet again,
missed another good nightly news story.

                                        over there,
                        alarm clocks must've not went off,
          so nobody woke up to make it to the site of busted up bodies
                              looking a lot like moon craters.
                    reporters must've lost their jobs for all their lateness
                                        and unwoken eyes.
                        i guess that's why i didn't see their stories in
                                        the new york times.
                    billions of ink print cartridges must've went empty,
                              so their stories never got printed.
                              i'm sure that was never the intent.

all i heard,
was she'd been runnin' round the block,
arms wrapped 'round the neighborhood sweethearts.
that she,
some militant dyke with gold plated teeth
and now,
her blood stained baggy pants sag six feet
below the earth's waist line.

                        twenty-four bullets to the back.
                              and all the blood,
                                    all cleaned up
                        before the photos made it to the internet.

25

of course there must've been witnesses
that witnessed her transition to spirit.
bystanders who took out their phones
                    with uncharged batteries
couldn't capture the beating –
no space for video recordings   too many selfies.
a hurried woman,
busy ordering deli sandwiches for a corporate party.

                              i think that day,
                    kim kardashian's ass broke the internet.
                    i'm sure had she not crashed the web
                    by poking at the ghost of sara baartman,
                        the outrage of the black community
                        would have blacked-out social media.

i think that day,
i musta been having a solo ceremony or something
saying to myself,
                    "Malissa Williams,
                    Sakia Gunn,
                    Kindra Chapman,
                    Crystal Jackson
ashe, ashe, ashe,"
but no other Black bodies were partaking in libation
mourning the falling queer bodies by police barrels
and vigilantes poppin shots in back shoulders.

i think that day,
all ears musta went deaf,
god musta pressed mute on all loose mouths
so all parted lips screaming   "please don't shoot!"
were not heard.

no one heard the catcalling on corners
by men
dying to penetrate butch bodies,
to show them "what they've been missing".
big fists to women's mouths with sounds of

> "you want to look like a man!?
> i will treat you like a man!"

went unheard that day.

i'm sure, had tanks been filled,
printers been printing,
phones been working,
feet been running to scenes,
and god would have not been playing god,
the world would've been outraged
by the deliberate erasure of black,

> butch,
> bodies

and our stories would've been heard.

... Sandra Bland, Ashe

pale skin yell *"i will light you up"*

i will take firearm to body
and leave you unbreathing
till breath is no longer able to talk back
to talk *Black*
to let full black lips talk sass.

Sandra Bland,
they wonder how you dare be Black woman

                with voice,

to know your rights,
to be angry,
to contest orders,
to demand our justice.
they think we too dark for freedom,
too Black woman for agency,
too nigger for breath.

Bland,
you are i
and i are you
call it suicide, call it murder
call it dangling

        from

          noose,

      fear of demanding already makes us strange fruit.

He/Him/His

He is concave back with palms swiping towards the earth,
his shoulders hold knapsacks of the girl in his body
                                        packed away,
his heart spills over his chest from lovers
                    that became ex-lovers
and I want to hold him, like any older sibling would.

his existence is ancient
though there's much erasure of his laboring hands
and the work they've done to nourish all bodies.

his palms:
lifelines moving in a gentle sway,
like trees catching wind in spring.
branches,
roots,
earth,
trees,
noose.
written there.

                    the swinging rope
                    a familiar worry
his freedom like at any moment i can get lynched for this,
like i can be rotten corpse   that wept
                dangling from trees
like saddened Sunday's,
like d r a g g e d by ankles to picnics,
death printed on postcards,
postmarked a c r o s s the country.
and still,
he cracks a smile through all the heartbreak,

all the erasure,
all the violent possibilities
and asserts his *new* pronouns: he/him/his
i think this is what freedom must look like.

.

when we think we are God
not their reflection,
but God themselves:
we can swallow our own violence
& call it martyrdom.
we can create genocide
& call it necessary.
we can terrorize
& call it justified.
it is then we can hate everything so deeply,
because we'd be our only reflection.

Dear Mama

Ma,
i don't think i told you enough how much i love you.
how i saw you carrying three children on your back
                    the world on your shoulders
                        dead babies in your belly
and still,
you kept moving in stilted strap-on heels,
Black god you are
how'd you do it?
i'm in awe you exist
                    black

                        and woman
with a certain grace i am not old enough to achieve yet.

this is the most painful conversation i will ever have
with a woman who will have my heart,
but what will you do when my body is made a carcass?
                    a decaying thing with no longer a fast mouth
                                        and
                                        loud
                                        skin
i was a dead girl before you birthed me into this world.

you gave birth to a body that was dead long before you birthed it
now i am being hunted down by white pigs in blue suits,
by white suits and holy crosses etched in gold,
                        sending me back
                    to where
                i came from.
so Ma,
have you already prepared yourself to see my skull cracked open?
you must've known our black asses were not welcome here.

will the images of how your child was brutally

                                        shot,
                                      killed,
                              shock you?

what will you do when the news headline says,
"woman killed by mentally ill man"
instead of
"girl murdered by state-sanctioned violence?"

pulse night club was shot up,
queer
colored
bodies heaved their last breath on a dance floor,
and you called me frantic,
asking me not to go to pride this year.
and like the headstrong child i've always been,
i told you

                    " i'm still going."

when you heard those words,
did you start planning my funeral?
did you imagine my bullet riddled body
                              covered in carnations?
did you know that was my favorite flower?

what will you do when my murderer is called a martyr?
                    said he did it in the name of religion?
              in the name of me not complying to a cop's order?
                    in the name of me resisting my rapist?
what will you do when the judge says *his* future
matters more than mine?

or when my story is reduced
to a hate crime
when it really was a genocide.

Mama,
these are things you and i must think about.

i used to wish i could closet my blackness
like i closeted my queerness.
i guess for a Black person,
being in a coffin is the closest thing
to being in the closet.

when they tell you i should've kept my mouth shut,
will you remind them,
mouth shut
hands up
unarmed
i could still kiss the mouth of a barrel?

so please still kiss me to sleep and tell me that you love me,
the world is breaking me.
but i have powerful ancestors,
and the arms of you,
and right now
that's all i need to carry me.

A Laying On of Hands

baldwin, lorde, hurston, hansberry, pat parker

                laid

                palms

                on my lower spine,

a rebirth ceremony of returning to the water,

a being a body immersed in all their sweat,

                in all their blood, in all their tears.

langston hughes offers his deep river waters to my mouth

for nourishment

                and i drink.

my body l e n g t h e n s,

                d e e p e n s,

                and e x p a n d s.

with my relatives in spirit holding me up

i dare to exist

to take   up   space

to be unapologetically myself in a skin

that reflects being under the brunt of brutality,

being pushed in corners and closets.

                that reflect generations of genocide.

let me show you this buoyant body

far from shrinking

from caved in shoulders

from buckled knees

from low-hung head

from shuffling in shoes

from being tight-lipped.

        wading.

i am always being carried.

black love in the midst of genocide
is a loophole white supremacy could *never*
get its hands on.

The Flood

her jaw drops in awe.

she goes into her bag,
pulls out her makeup mirror,
and holds it between my legs.

"i want you to see yourself;
 your djembe pulse;
watch your rhythm flood us."

A Black Feminist Love Poem

i am the resurgence of my abducted ancestry –
all noose, chain, whipped words –

                           they tried to beat the hell out of me.
the innocent cry of a child who'd grow
to only be known as chattel.
a marginalized people deemed uneducable.
unapologetic me,
speaking my black low class tongue –
raging tongue so sharp cut like knife
to any fucker who dare say sumn sexist.
my tongue be a Black feminist
walking in imprints of bell hooks.
my tongue can be weapon against whiteness
or white flag
         when i let love in.

watch my militant words wash away
when her arms enfold me
my guard gates subside in the presence
                of this riotous woman.
she,
a burning riot riled up underneath her skin
black fist clenched to the sky with left foot leading
her heart is the spearhead of her frontline revolution
she is like a young kathleen cleaver reincarnated
with laced dr. martens pressed into patriarchy's thick skull.

and i love how her stature melts and contorts
when i take my fingertips to the back of her scalp
and momentarily dissipate her militancy
as i make waves throughout her hair

and her body
            sinks
                    into my soul.

four months ago,
we'd find ourselves in the middle of a forest
being swallowed by redwoods.
thick trunks surround us like sara baartman specters.
leaves fell from arms as if trying to get closer
to our exchanging of secrets
with the black sky's infinite eyes as our witness
i told you that i love you.
that i've always had my eyes on you like overseer oversee
that you leave me unbreathing
                    like necks
                            hung from trees.
and we'd lean in and kiss each other for the first time
and in your presence,
i no longer felt like 3/5ths human.

i can still hear the rhythm of your heartbeat
pounding on my chest from the first time we made love
two black skinned babes lay bodied to bodied
                    vulnerable,
                            unafraid,
eye witnesses to each other's unkempt wilderness
between legs
like unclipped bouquets.

i swore i could hear our ancestors shout
through the pulsation of our riotous song
no drums could ever imagine sounding more profound
than the pounding of our hearts beating
and in that moment you and i were nothing short

of the greatest sound ever created.
sweet moans between two black bodies

                    how dare that be so revolutionary?

they say,
generational trauma lie somewhere in our backbones
i'm sure my insatiable longing for you
                is the residual effect of the forbiddingness
of two black women to be in love
while enslaved:
master made our bodies a property,
a commodity,
made you: maid, servant, domesticated, enslaved
made me: all-crimpled, thistled-finger, hunched back,

                                  picking cotton
you: all legs spread out open to white man invasion
they tried white-washing your Afrikan lineage,
you golden dipped Afrikan queen,
made you birth other mulatto babies
that look nothing like me –
all-ebony, sun-scorched, long-houred, back-blistered,
caved in shoulders
they said that we
              you and i,
could be nothing more than a division
of house   and field.

and i'm sure,
in our past life you must have caught a glance of me
                  outside of colonized windows
and i may have seen you in there wearing white sundresses
so beautifully
wanting nothing more than to escape with you
in the deep dark wilderness

away from this plantation,

maybe back then you and i actually did

could that be why four months ago
our first kiss happened

in the middle of a forest?

Polyamory

polyamory,

because too often has my love been mistaken
for sexual exclusivity.

i am deeply committed to fostering trust
and sustaining loverships rooted in kindness,

                        transparency,
                        accountability,

&
absolute
freedom.

These Hoes

a colonized tongue says,
"you can't turn a hoe into a housewife."
the colonizer responds
"but, you can turn her into a house nigger"
together they say,

> *"i meaaan, these hoes got bodies that be*
> *open, available, loose."*

pause,

to loose-laced Afrikan garment draped in the motherland
they saw us as hoes since they laid eyes
on our black ancestral mothers
clad appropriately for sub-saharan weather.

our Black women –

magical misses
shaman
priestess
praise dances
rites and rituals
herbal healers
black magic
witch-crafting
beauty.
a breath of God herself,
stolen and exploited for the sacred
magic tween her thighs.

they cared not that she, birthed origin
her hands, cultivator of all life that grows from this soil

still, they call her "hoe" by default
an open invitation
like,

> *"you are cordially invited*
> *to buy this black body off the block,*
> *it can birth other bodies*
> *that we make commodity.*

> *it ain't* **rape** *if we call her merely,* **property"**

there, it begins,
the Black woman not being capable of giving of consent.

i guess that's why when a Black woman is raped

her story is not a tragedy.
is not a bang of a gavel
is not an indictment
is not an excuse for mourning
but a forcing to be resilient.

"pick yourself up"
"look at how strong she be"
how she is never allocated "victimhood"
how she will be called a "survivor"

before she is able
to feel to be one
herself.

Yemaya,

to be swallowed by you would've been a mercy killing
                    your unrelenting wave crashing shore
                                        devouring me.
                                    return me home.
i heard there's life at the bottom of the ocean.

A Stool Under The Hanging Rope

it's like a suicide letter inscribed only in your frontal lobe
pen to paper defeats the purpose of silent suffering.
are we all always hanging rope under cap skull,
lynching any thinking thoughts that say we are as great as we are
told?

fourteen-feet below my ashen-cracked swollen soles,
lay buried feminist politics of,

    "hey victims do not blame yourself,
     you shattered soft butterfly wing
     knocked by entitled wind blow"
but i knew i could have flown away faster.
i know i'm supposed to know it wasn't my fault
that entry with force opened me up in places i cautiously kept
closed
that when i cried

 no

  stop

   this hurts

    you're breaking my body
this marble pillar crumbling away from acid rain
he shudda got up offa me
got his dick up outta me
didn't he feel my pelvic bones cracking to dust?
dusted box tucked in closets,
not never letting even lovers dust me off.

my vagina: cobweb coated,
anansi occupied, faint whisper of past invasion, ghosted,
unalive, ungraciously fed on by ghoul.
but i blamed myself.

submerging in alcoholic water
shot, after shot, after shot, until i stumble into incoherency and
blackness, off-balance
i blame it on my suppression
of my secret longing of male affection
blame it on too many guards i have on guard against men
did i come off as too standoffish?
     did my masculinity offend them?
          did it tongue a language to their hormones
          that i was needing of some sorry sort
               of male intervention?

i, too prude, perhaps,
     kinky killjoy
santa cruz sexual revolutionist kids – anything goes here
this is free flying hippy shit
should i have been okay with this sort of liberation?
watching him be reborn in his sexual awakening.
i know i'm supposed to know this black body
has never been my property
so how could i expect a running to my rescue
when there is no such thing as a Black woman's innocence?
even when she cries songs of pain,
like a chattel child would.

cracked mouth opens wide,
and like any feminist say,
i tell you,
     "i know it wasn't my fault."

but a stool
        kicks
           over
              under the hanging rope

another internal lynching of that thought.

lifeless they all swing.

                                    and you'll never see
this letter written out on paper.

Stop,
Somebody turn the light on
Cause I can't see life without you.
My heart, my soul,
It bleeds for you.
Every night I pray for you,
I ask God to cover you,
If that's not enough,
I sit down and meditate for you.
If you don't believe that, Cierra,
Look up at that star,
Cause that star shines bright for you.

Jolinda, Mama

I was reaching towards the firmament
In a flask of fermented fruits.

Funambulist

"The only place I feel alive", said Karl Wallenda, "is on the wire." And there he was this morning: seventy-three years old, one-hundred and twenty feet in the air, ten stories above San Juan, performing as he had done for fifty-eight years, walking a tightrope from one beach hotel to another.
As he reached halfway, the ocean wind gust to thirty knots, and Karl Wallenda, the best man in the world for walking on wires, fought for his balance

> but
> plunged.

Two-hundred people saw him fall,
rushed to help,
but it was too late.

"The only place I feel alive", I said, "is on the wire." And there I was that day, twenty-one years old, feet planted on the ground, thousands of feet below a God all-seeing , seven shots deep in a bottle I had no intentions of sharing,
and I was performing, just like I had learned to do since alcohol became accessible.

Funambulism is the art of walking along a thin wire or rope, also known as tightrope-walking, commonly associated with the circus.

My mother said I was breached, born upside-down with my feet trying to get out first. I'd grow to a child who'd put toothpaste on quarters, and squeeze the iron-mint concoction in my hands while I sat on the toilet. My brother would call me "gay" as a joke, before I knew it to actually be true (because he is clairvoyant and amazing). And I'd quickly learned that to be Black and queer in the suburbs is to grow up feeling like a circus freak. To be the only queer body in heteronormative spaces, especially Black spaces where you are seen as a derailment to Black liberation,

is to always feel like you do not belong.

Every party became my tightrope.

Saturday nights the audience conjured in compact places with body counts exceeding the room's capacity. Ass being thrown by the Black girls, and all the Black boys too scared to catch it, so the girls dance with themselves. And me, well, as coy introvert Capricorns do be, I'd spend hours finding courage to dance, to live, to be. The street corner store packaged courage in a bottle and you'd catch me in the corners dancing with vodka until lights down.

My world goes Blackout. Blank. Showtime.

When I was a child, Papa would come home late at night,
With limbs that didn't seem like they belonged to him,
Like a body trying to keep balance against wind gusting at thirty-plus knots. My brother, sister, and I watched in painful awe, hoping he would make it across the hall
without making a bloodstained carpet out of our mother.

He is performing
And he is laughing,
Inebriated laughter,
A mockery of himself.
A tightrope walking master.
Teach me what courage look like.

Fast forward to the lights going up, my tightrope act over,
To being told the ticket price was worth the show.
That I was wildin' out, captured on recording,
Entertaining two-hundred people

> on edge
> waiting to witness

> > > a downfall
> that would be too late to remediate.

& the show flew by, not ever remembering what happened
during.

In the events recounting,
I'd hear stories of my contemplation to completely jump, of
unrecognizable rage, of being emotionally unlocked, of loose-
limb dancing, of public spectacle, of non-consensual
groping of others and kiss begging – *please*,
of *fuck me* to invisible boys whose names I do not know.

& the me awake, grew resentment for the me, asleep.
the me deeply craving intimacy, grew resentment for the me
confusing it with sex and kissing.
& the me wanting to be loved, couldn't muster compassion for
the pain experienced by disappointed lovers I disregarded in my
pursuits.

To tightrope is to be a balancing act of thrilling moments and
broken bones. A balance act of self-control and losing it all. Is to
act and always be susceptible

> > To fall

> To crash

> > To die,

But death don't always mean you die.

When people asked why I would be entering a Twelve Step

program at age twenty-two,
I say,
"Because I have watched too many deaths,
To not turn this one into a rebirth.
Because inherited cycles can always end with me.
Because to say no to alcohol
And how it makes a boundary – invading me
    Is to always be accountable to myself
    Is to be accountable to pain I inflict onto others
        Is to say Yes to ancestral love,
            Yes to community love,
            Yes to Black love,
            Which is to say,
                Yes to self-love.

Step 1

i am powerless over alcohol
& my life has become unmanageable

The Coosa River's toothless jaw and salivating lips
Carry engraved tombstones and entire cemeteries

                                                    submerged

Histories, legacies, of plantation, of bone, of flesh,
Make river floors
Symphony, hymn of young Black girl's laughter & wit
& Church bell, make ripple and current through the waters
The waters that tasted of petrified sweat and sob
When the river dam broke.

Ain't nothing can keep the waters from runnin.

The Ghosts of My Past Live in My Body Waters

i do not wanna let my waters run
i do not wanna let my waters run
i do not wanna let my waters run
i do not wanna let my   waters   run
i do not wanna let my   waters   run
i do not wanna let my   waters   run
i do not wanna let my   waters   run
i do not wanna let my   waters   run
i do not   wanna   let my   waters   run
i do not wanna let my waters   run
i do not wanna l   et my waters   run
i do not wanna let my waters   run
i do not wanna let my waters   run
i do not wanna let my waters   run
i do not wanna let my waters   run
i do not wanna let my waters   run
i do not wanna let   my waters   run
i do not wan na let my wa   ters   run
i do not wa nna let my wat ers   run
i do not wa nna   let my w   a   ters   run

                                        runnin', gotta keep runnin'
                                        runnin', gotta keep runnin'
                                        runnin', gotta keep runnin'
                                        runnin', gotta keep runnin'
                                        runnin', gotta keep runnin'

When the Dam Breaks

My brother mocks the ash on my kneecaps
Say "Heh, it look like Pookie lips from New Jack City"
Before Mama say "Lil girl put some lotion on them legs"
The musky scent festering in my underarms follow me out the
front door
I be the Black girl that play basketball in cowboy boots
& I am unbothered
The boys still can't catch me.

I be seven-years-old and be the fastest-bestest runner in the first
grade.
The Pink barrettes enclosing my pigtails-
Weaved by Mama Ja'Queen's dark black hands
Blow off, slicing the wind behind me.
The sweat makes my slicked edges raise defying gravity
And I am scuffed boot and K-Swiss sneaker
Kissed with field grass and playground pavement
That Mama go make me clean with toothbrush and soap
When I get back home.

But for now, wild I run
The organisms of my body rush and sweep past leaning
tetherball poles
A young running Black girl,
A river, raging,
howling "catch me if you can
But you can't catch me huh,
you can't catch me."

I wet my lips for the first time,
A young Black boy say,

"Here take a swig of this,
It's cheap but it sho' do the job.
This shit right here, this shit right here.
A dam that close the floodgates,
Keeps all the ghosts in your river at bay
Say,
You don't gotta deal with all your waters at once."

With each shot,
I felt the installation of each cement block build within me
It barricaded
The violence, the torment, the self-doubt, the hate
The repulsion for my flesh, and bone, and skin
Every gulp from the rim of the bottle electrified me
Padlocked the pain
Memories became manageable
Trauma became trivial
I became invincible.

When the dam breaks
Which is always *Will*
If made by mortals,
Silence will ensue as if to not have seen the warning signs
Of a stone wall caving in on itself
Shattering all the mechanisms built to keep the water out.

When the stark silence crept over the eruption
And I laid open, covered in the depths of my blue,
God revealed themselves, vantablack
Bursting a core of Alona Jean light, warming my spine.

My God,
They were not in a bottle
They were not white nor man

They were not Black nor woman
They were as complex as the gender that
Never feels right on my tongue
When I try to give it name,
Which is to say water is spirit
Is ghost, Is God
Is ancestor, Is trauma
Is healing, Is recovery
Is running
Is always replenishing itself, holy.

I resuscitate the girl in my body I blocked away
I cannot avoid her tears and wail
Sending ripple through *our* body
Tell her she's loved
She's seen
& I take rebuilding Us a day at a time.
Tell her, Cierra
I am in awe of you
How you awaken in the morning,
Lace your shoes and remind me
The door is always ours to run through.

Runnin', Gotta Keep

Runnin', Gotta Keep Runnin'
Runnin', Gotta Keep Runnin'
Runnin', Gotta Keep Runnin'

HELLO CIERRA,
HAPPY FREEDOM.

Afterword

I often conjure an image of baby Cierra in my mind, she's standing eager-ready, with a long extended neck and a face covered mostly with a huge smile; I imagine she'd been singing *cheeeeese* in a key that probably parted the heart of Mama and Papa who snapped the photo. This baby, this beautiful Black child, I say to myself, how could I ever do anything other than love her, fiercely, and I am careful with words I say to myself because she is always listening. I am also watching my inner teenage boi soften, I tell them that they no longer have to perform masculinity as a survival mechanism, tell them *we are safe now*, and they cradle baby Cierra in the moments I forget that having a relationship with myself requires *daily* maintenance.

Falling in love with myself, as a reflection of God, is a continual process and I am in awe at the love that is conjured in moments of stillness, meditation, prayer, daily gratitude lists, and one-on-ones with those I love dearly. I am overflowing with forgiveness for my younger selves wading in the ways we knew how, while holding radical compassion for the future lessons brewed from our imperfections.

Accountability, too, is a process of learning and unlearning, and the ways I hold myself accountable to others is entirely dependent on what accountability looks like for them; this is a process that I neither run from, nor cower to. Accountability, to myself, is not possible without making a lifelong commitment to sobriety, though I take it a day at a time, and through making a commitment to mothering my inner children so together, we never mistake ourselves as anything other than worthy, adequate, and capable of coping fully with life on life's terms.

About the Author

 Cierra Green, Bobbi Kindred, Jolinda's baby, and Storyteller, because there are multiple energetic beings that exist within Them and each must be honored. They deeply believe in the power of storytelling to heal the inner child and it is how they honor the wounds within themselves that still gape. Through storytelling, they invoke the spirit of their ancestors' tongue when they share communally. They are peppermint oil to the scalp regiment, and ukulele pluck to "Fast Car"—Tracy Chapman on mornings with room for ruminating, and "Just a Girl" on karaoke nights when singing off key matters less than putting on an honest show.

They are a former resident of the Destiny Arts Center's Queer Emerging Artist Residency in Oakland, CA., and their work has been featured at venues such as The Berkeley Group Reparatory Theater, The Impact Hub Oakland, and Intersection for the Arts in San Francisco. They have slammed at the College Unions Poetry Slam Invitational (CUPSI 2016) in Austin, Texas, and are a contracted actor for Berkeley Reparatory Theater's Young Writers of Color Collective. They are in a touring production of Ntozake Shange's "*For Colored Girls Who Have Considered Suicide When the Rainbow is Enuf*" and are a member of the performing arts and writing collective, *Fine Ass Queer Artsy Heauxs Collective* who is responsible for the production *"The Niggas Speak of Rivers"* directed by Lisa Evans. They are also the newest member of poetry collective, *Pr3ssPlay Poets,* whose stage production "*The State of Black Bodies*", directed by Mona Webb, was featured at the National Queer Arts Festival, Oakland, 2018. Connect with the author: thisboiyantbody@gmail.com.

Made in the USA
Columbia, SC
13 September 2020